The dying Christian's triumph in a living redeemer exemplified in a sermon, preached at Sutton in Ashfield, Nottinghamshire, occasioned by the death of Matthew Butcher, jun. who departed this life, December 10, 1777, aged 22 years. By John Barrett.

John Barrett

ECCO
PRINT EDITIONS

The dying Christian's triumph in a living redeemer exemplified in a sermon, preached at Sutton in Ashfield, Nottinghamshire, occasioned by the death of Matthew Butcher, jun. who departed this life, December 10, 1777, aged 22 years. By John Barrett.

Barrett, John
ESTCID: T074221
Reproduction from British Library

[London] : Printed by A. Bell, London; and sold by Joseph Heath, Nottingham and Mansfield, [1778?].
48p. ; 8°

Eighteenth Century
Collections Online
Print Editions

Gale ECCO Print Editions

Relive history with *Eighteenth Century Collections Online*, now available in print for the independent historian and collector. This series includes the most significant English-language and foreign-language works printed in Great Britain during the eighteenth century, and is organized in seven different subject areas including literature and language; medicine, science, and technology; and religion and philosophy. The collection also includes thousands of important works from the Americas.

The eighteenth century has been called "The Age of Enlightenment." It was a period of rapid advance in print culture and publishing, in world exploration, and in the rapid growth of science and technology – all of which had a profound impact on the political and cultural landscape. At the end of the century the American Revolution, French Revolution and Industrial Revolution, perhaps three of the most significant events in modern history, set in motion developments that eventually dominated world political, economic, and social life.

In a groundbreaking effort, Gale initiated a revolution of its own: digitization of epic proportions to preserve these invaluable works in the largest online archive of its kind. Contributions from major world libraries constitute over 175,000 original printed works. Scanned images of the actual pages, rather than transcriptions, recreate the works *as they first appeared.*

Now for the first time, these high-quality digital scans of original works are available via print-on-demand, making them readily accessible to libraries, students, independent scholars, and readers of all ages.

For our initial release we have created seven robust collections to form one the world's most comprehensive catalogs of 18th century works.

Initial Gale ECCO Print Editions collections include:

History and Geography
Rich in titles on English life and social history, this collection spans the world as it was known to eighteenth-century historians and explorers. Titles include a wealth of travel accounts and diaries, histories of nations from throughout the world, and maps and charts of a world that was still being discovered. Students of the War of American Independence will find fascinating accounts from the British side of conflict.

Social Science

Delve into what it was like to live during the eighteenth century by reading the first-hand accounts of everyday people, including city dwellers and farmers, businessmen and bankers, artisans and merchants, artists and their patrons, politicians and their constituents. Original texts make the American, French, and Industrial revolutions vividly contemporary.

Medicine, Science and Technology

Medical theory and practice of the 1700s developed rapidly, as is evidenced by the extensive collection, which includes descriptions of diseases, their conditions, and treatments. Books on science and technology, agriculture, military technology, natural philosophy, even cookbooks, are all contained here.

Literature and Language

Western literary study flows out of eighteenth-century works by Alexander Pope, Daniel Defoe, Henry Fielding, Frances Burney, Denis Diderot, Johann Gottfried Herder, Johann Wolfgang von Goethe, and others. Experience the birth of the modern novel, or compare the development of language using dictionaries and grammar discourses.

Religion and Philosophy

The Age of Enlightenment profoundly enriched religious and philosophical understanding and continues to influence present-day thinking. Works collected here include masterpieces by David Hume, Immanuel Kant, and Jean-Jacques Rousseau, as well as religious sermons and moral debates on the issues of the day, such as the slave trade. The Age of Reason saw conflict between Protestantism and Catholicism transformed into one between faith and logic -- a debate that continues in the twenty-first century.

Law and Reference

This collection reveals the history of English common law and Empire law in a vastly changing world of British expansion. Dominating the legal field is the *Commentaries of the Law of England* by Sir William Blackstone, which first appeared in 1765. Reference works such as almanacs and catalogues continue to educate us by revealing the day-to-day workings of society.

Fine Arts

The eighteenth-century fascination with Greek and Roman antiquity followed the systematic excavation of the ruins at Pompeii and Herculaneum in southern Italy; and after 1750 a neoclassical style dominated all artistic fields. The titles here trace developments in mostly English-language works on painting, sculpture, architecture, music, theater, and other disciplines. Instructional works on musical instruments, catalogs of art objects, comic operas, and more are also included.

The BiblioLife Network

This project was made possible in part by the BiblioLife Network (BLN), a project aimed at addressing some of the huge challenges facing book preservationists around the world. The BLN includes libraries, library networks, archives, subject matter experts, online communities and library service providers. We believe every book ever published should be available as a high-quality print reproduction; printed on-demand anywhere in the world. This insures the ongoing accessibility of the content and helps generate sustainable revenue for the libraries and organizations that work to preserve these important materials.

The following book is in the "public domain" and represents an authentic reproduction of the text as printed by the original publisher. While we have attempted to accurately maintain the integrity of the original work, there are sometimes problems with the original work or the micro-film from which the books were digitized. This can result in minor errors in reproduction. Possible imperfections include missing and blurred pages, poor pictures, markings and other reproduction issues beyond our control. Because this work is culturally important, we have made it available as part of our commitment to protecting, preserving, and promoting the world's literature.

GUIDE TO FOLD-OUTS MAPS and OVERSIZED IMAGES

The book you are reading was digitized from microfilm captured over the past thirty to forty years. Years after the creation of the original microfilm, the book was converted to digital files and made available in an online database.

In an online database, page images do not need to conform to the size restrictions found in a printed book. When converting these images back into a printed bound book, the page sizes are standardized in ways that maintain the detail of the original. For large images, such as fold-out maps, the original page image is split into two or more pages

Guidelines used to determine how to split the page image follows:

• Some images are split vertically; large images require vertical and horizontal splits.
• For horizontal splits, the content is split left to right.
• For vertical splits, the content is split from top to bottom.
• For both vertical and horizontal splits, the image is processed from top left to bottom right.

The Dying Christian's Triumph

IN A

LIVING REDEEMER

EXEMPLIFIED IN A

SERMON,

PREACHED AT SUTTON IN ASHFIELD,

NOTTINGHAMSHIRE,

OCCASIONED BY THE DEATH OF

MATTHEW BUTCHER, JUN.

WHO DEPARTED THIS LIFE, DECEMBER 10, 1777,

AGED 22 YEARS.

BY *JOHN BARRETT.*

But why more Woe? more Comfort let it be.
Nothing is dead, but that which wish'd to die.
Nothing is dead, but Wretchedness and Pain.
Nothing is dead, but what encumber'd, gall'd,
Block'd up the Pass, and barr'd from real Life.

YOUNG.

Printed by A. BELL, No. 8, ALDGATE, LONDON;
And fold by JOSEPH HEATH, Bookseller,
NOTTINGHAM and MANSFIELD.

A

SERMON, &c.

I AM now entering on the moſt painful employment in which I ever was engaged. The powerful feelings of friendſhip in buſy exerciſe afflict my ſoul with the moſt oppreſſive ſorrow. Unleſs reſtrained by an inviſible hand, my overpowering paſſions will ſtop my mouth, and cauſe me to leave the pulpit in gloomy ſilence.

What encourages me to beg your intereſt for me at a throne of grace is a firm belief that the ſame ſorrow is univerſal throughout this aſſembly; and I would

therefore

therefore hope that, while you tenderly drop the tear of affection on your own account, you will fervently whifper a prayer on mine, that ftrength may be equal to my day, and utterance may be given me to improve this hour of diftrefs by confidering that portion of the divine word contained in

Job, Chap. xix. Verfe 25, 26, 27.

For I know that my Redeemer liveth, and that he fhall fland at the latter day upon the earth: and though after my fkin worms deftroy this body, yet in my flefh fhall I fee God, whom I fhall fee for myfelf, and mine eyes fhall behold, and not another; though my reins be confumed within me.

When an old houfe is to be broken up, and a new one built in its place, the perfon who refides in it has warning from his landlord to remove, while the old habitation is taken down and another erected. Something fimilar to this is the fituation of God's people in a dying hour. The natural body, that

that earthly houfe of this our tabernacle is
then to be diffolved or taken down, in or-
der that it may be built anew, and raifed
a glorious body. For a time therefore
its tenant, the immortal fpirit, muft forfake her clay and leave her old habitation ;
and though the event frequently may
come unnoticed, and the foul may make
a fudden unexpected departure, this is very
far from being always the cafe: fome bodily
complaint or another is ufually fent to
warn us of the momentous change, and intimate our approaching diffolution. Accordingly in this light it was that afflicted *Job* confidered the painful diforder under which he now laboured. Though it
was not followed immediately by his
death, it informed him that the ghaftly
meffenger was on the road, and warned
him of his approach. In confequence of
fuch a warning he utters the language of
the text, which defcribes him in the realizing views of this gloomy fcene. Simi-
lar were the views, and more explicit was
the warning received by my dear departed
friend. The complaint under which he

laboured

laboured not only informed him (like *Job*) that he muſt die in ſome future period, but it told him in the language of certainty, the hour was at hand. He knew that there was but a ſtep between him and death, yet inſtead of trembling before the pale deſtroyer, ſo dreadful to nature, with an undaunted courage he looked him in the face. He ſaw in him the countenance of a friend, and gave him a chearful hearty welcome. The reaſon was, almighty grace enabled him to behold a riſen Saviour, and therefore, ſtrong in faith, he could adopt the language of my text, and ſay, *I know that my Redeemer liveth*. Accordingly a paper found on the morning of his death, directed for me, and written juſt before his departure, expreſſes his deſire that the verſes I have read ſhould be the foundation of my diſcourſe on the preſent melancholy occaſion.

Theſe words may properly be ſtyled a compendious body of doctrinal and experimental divinity. They contain the ſum and ſubſtance of all divine revelation, while

they

they breathe the very effence of the chriftian's experience, when faith is in lively exercife. The ideas with which they are fraught are fo numerous, and the language fo fublime, that in one difcourfe it is impoffible to unfold all their beauties. I fhall only therefore touch upon the feveral parts of my text, by collecting them together in the three following points of view.

I. A confeffion of mortality; *Though after my fkin worms deftroy this body; though my reins are confumed within me.*

II. A profeffion of faith; *I know that my Redeemer liveth, and that he fhall ftand at the latter day upon the earth.*

III. A declaration of hope; *Yet in my flefh fhall I fee God, whom I fhall fee for myfelf, mine eyes, fhall behold and not another.*

I. A confeffion of mortality ; *Though after my fkin, &c.* Death, confidered only as a matter of fpeculation, is that important event which affords the moft convincing teftimony how greatly our nature is depraved. Its certainty is univerfally ac-

acknowledged

knowledged, but the generality of man-kind reflect on it with indifference, while each individual confiders the diffolution of another more than his own. Indeed, to nature there is fomething fo painful in the thought, that none but the real-believer, under the influence of divine grace, can bear to indulge it. Such a one was the dear deceafed, and therefore with *Job* he could utter the language I have read as expreffive of the following particulars.

I. His realizing views of the natural confequences of death. *Though after my fkin worms deftroy this body.* The expref-fion points to the remote confequence of nature's diffolution, and defcribes its moft ruinous ftate. *Though after my fkin worms deftroy this body, (i. e.)* "After the pale "hand of death has changed my counte-"nance, and the grave's cold damps have "penetrated my fkin, putrified it, and "altered its whole appearance, *then worms* "*fhall deftroy this body.*" In fuch a ftate as this, the pleafure which once was felt by furviving friends is changed for dif-guft.

guft. The tendereft relative turns away his eyes from the loathfome object, while none but the worms embrace it with delight. Thus confuming in the grave the greedy reptiles feaft themfelves on the putrified carcafe till they have devoured its laft remains.

Such, fays *Job*, will foon be the wretched condition of this my body. The word *body*, you may remark, is written in *italics* to intimate it is not in the original. When read without it, the expreffion is truly defcriptive, and conveys the moft lively image of the good man's fituation. It reprefents him (as it were) pointing with his finger to his emaciated carcafe, while he thus expreffes himfelf, *Though after my fkin worms deftroy* THIS; fo vile and defpicable does it appear, that it hardly deferves a name, and it will foon be treated with fuitable contempt, while every once lively member, every once active limb lie dormant in the grave, and are configned to corruption. Another thing implied in this expreffion is,

B   IIdly.

IIdly, the certainty of this event. *Though after my skin worms destroy this body.* You will observe in this expression death is not asserted, but implied *Job* does not say that he shall die, but intimates his undoubted assurance of his death by taking it as a truth for granted. The fact was so indisputably true that it needed no proof, he therefore speaks of it in the same manner as though it was actually past. He realizes the dismal scene, as if the event had really taken place, and supposes himself in the humiliating situation described in the expression. *Though after my skin worms destroy this body.*

IIIdly. In the words, *though after my skin worms destroy this body, and though my reins are consumed within me,* we have the reason of the certainty of his dissolution. Human depravity is the foundation upon which death hath raised its empire. The declarations of Scripture, and the mortality of those around us afford convincing arguments that its dominion is universal, and none are exempted from its destructive blow,

blow; but thefe general reafons only dif-
covei the certainty of our diffolution in
common with others, and are equally con-
clufive with refpect to all mankind, but
the particular caufe of *Job*'s affuiance in
the prefent cafe feems to be the peculiar
circumftances he was now in as an afflicted
man. thefe he expreffes in verfe 27. *my
reins are confumed within me.* The dreadful difoider with which he was afflicted
feemed to have eaten up his veiy vitals.
The pains attending it enfeebled his
whole frame, as introducing him to the
chambers of death. Under his affliction
he *felt himfelf mortal*, he knew, if it con-
tinued, his diffolution muft enfue, and
read, as it were, the fentence of death
within himfelf. Thus, *his reins being confumed within him* teftified the certainty of
death, and opened his eyes to fee the hide-
ous confequences that muft neceffarily
follow. Such were his prefent circumftances as drew a veil over the face of natuie,
and rendered gloomy its brighteft objects.
The fcene of futurity which they piefent-
ed interpofed and concealed fiom his view
the

the fplendor of all earthly delights. In fuch a ftate he was conftrained to apply to heaven for relief, and abfolute mifery muft have excited the groans of defpair had not a divine friendfhip appeared on his behalf. To this therefore he applies for fupport and confolation, nor was his application in vain, as will evidently appear, if we confider,

IIdly. A profeffion of his faith. *I know that my Redeemer liveth, and that he fhall ftand at the latter day upon the earth.*

Thefe words evidently exprefs what was the object of the faith of *Job*, and defcribe thofe effential characteriftics in the perfon of Chrift, which convince the enlightened foul, that it enjoys a fuitable and all-fufficient Redeemer. It is a good obfervation which I remember to have had from an able divine, " Every finner needs a Redeemer, " and every chriftian has one." A conviction of our being in the number of the former neceffarily excites our defire to enjoy the bleffednefs of the latter. Thus it was in the cafe before us. *Job* was fully
convinced

convinced of his own vilenefs, he was
affured that fin was the caufe of natural
death, and he alfo knew that it expofed
him to eternal death ; confidering himfelf
therefore on this account as entiiely loft
and helplefs the only fource of his confolation was the method of redemption plan-
ned and executed by God himfelf. That
this merciful fcheme was revealed to him,
and that he underftood its nature is evi-
dent fiom the character by which he defcribes the object of his faith, as,

1ft. He was a Redeemei, *I know that
my Redeemer liveth.* The objections that
are urged to prove thefe words have no
reference to the perfon of Chrift are too
trivial, and too plainly confuted by the
whole ftrain of the text to need a particular attention on this folemn occafion.
I fhall only obferve in general that the
Hebrew word here ufed גאל contains an
allufion to a well known cuftom obferved
under the ceremonial law *(viz.)* when a
perfon was dead, whofe eftate was fold or
mortgaged, the neareft furviving kinfman
was to fettle his concerns, and maintain
the

the honour of the deceafed by redeeming the eftate, marrying the widow, and raifing up children to his name. We have an inftance of this in *Ruth*, chap. 4. where *Boaz* is defcribed as purchafing the eftate of *Mahlon*, and taking the wife of the dead to raife up the name of the dead upon his inheritance. The reafon of this tranfaction he acknowledges, in verfe 12 of the former chapter, to be the relation in which he ftood, when he fays, *And now it is true I am thy near kinfman.* You will obferve, it was this that qualified him for the bufinefs, and rendered him a fuitable Redeemer. Now it is the very fame word ufed in the text by which fuch a Redeemer is defcribed. Chrift bears the fame title becaufe he ftands in a fimilar relation, and does the fame kind fervice for his people.

1. He ftands in a fimilar relation to them. Accordingly he is defcribed in Scripture as our elder brother, bone of our bone, and flefh of our flefh. On this account the right of redemption belongs to him in a legal way as the proper fubftitute of his people. When Chrift hung

upon

upon the crofs at *Calvary* the fame nature which had finned was then fuffer-
ing, the threatenings of the divine law
were thus fulfilled, the faithfulnefs of the
law-giver was by this mean maintained,
and juftice received ample fatisfaction.
See this point argued by the apoftle in
Hebrews, chap. ii. from the 11th to verfe
18th, " For both he that fanctifieth," &c.

2. The Lord Jefus Chrift by his obe-
dience and death accomplifhed the fame
important work for his people, and therefore may be ftiled their kinfman, their
redeemer. By the fall we had fold ourfelves to work wickednefs, and became
the miferable fubjects of fin, and vaffals
of Satan. Chrift redeems the mortgage,
reftores the poffeffion, and fecures the
eternal honour of thofe who are dead in
fin. This he does in the fame manner as
Boaz did as to the eftate of *Mahlon* {*viz.*}
by paying its proper price. What this
was you may fee by reading I. *Peter*,
chap. i. verfes 18 and 19. " For we are
" not redeemed with corruptible things, as
" filver and gold, but with the precious
" blood

" blood of Jefus, as of a lamb without
" blemifh and without fpot." Such was
the price paid down for our redemption,
the value of which can only be eftima-
ted by an infinite mind, as appears from an
attentive reflection on the apoftolic affertion, Acts xx. 28. " Feed the church of
" God, which he hath purchafed with his
" own blood."

II. He was a living Redeemer. *I know
that my Redeemer liveth.* This was *Job's*
confolation, that there was not only a Redeemer to appear in fome future period,
but that he was at that very inftant actually in being. If the exiftence of Chrift
was only to be dated from the time in
which he took upon him our nature, then
the Old Teftament faints muft have pe-
rifhed for want of prefent relief. *Job*
felt the weight of his guilt in fuch a
manner, as convinced him he muft fink
under the enormous load, unlefs there was
one to interpofe with God in his behalf.
This therefore we find was the matter of
his wifh in chap. xvi. verfe 21. " O that
" one

" one might plead for a man with God,
" as a man pleadeth for his neighbour."
Divine grace taught him that such a one
was ready for the work, whilst it led him
to *Jesus*, the only mediator between God
and man. This therefore was the matter
of his rejoicing, when he says, in the
words of our text, " I know that my
" Redeemer liveth!" Observe, though
Christ had not suffered, yet he was then
in existence. What is more, he then
lived as the Redeemer of his people. In
this character he was set up from ever-
lasting. Hence the believer derives all
his consolation in the views of death.
Christ is a life-giving head. He lives
himself, and from him the springs of
eternal life flow in endless streams to all
his people. His character of a Redeemer
intimates that compassion, care, and friend-
ship, which he continually bears to his
church. His living implies that he is
at present, and will be in every future moment continually engaged in the exercise of
this his affection. As his love constrain-
ed him to become our Redeemer by dying

C   for

for us, fo it ftill influences him continually to act in the fame character by living for us. "He ever liveth therefore fays "the apoftle to make interceffion for us, "Hebrews vii. 25." Confequently he is always ready at the right hand of God to interpofe in our behalf; nor will he fuffer any one concern of his people to pafs unnoticed, any accufation againft them to be fuccefsful, or any injury defigned them to be accomplifhed.

How clearly does this difcover the fecurity of the child of God! To fpeak it with reverence, Chrift would appear difhonorable under the character of a Redeemer, if, while he fuftained it, one of his people was to be overcome by Satan, or perifh under the influence of fin. Nor need we fear in the profpect of death, or tremble at natuie's diffolution, fince Scripture reveals a living Redeemer as the object of our faith. Though this body is imprifoned in the grave, crumbled into duft, and devoured by worms, not one atom fhall be loft, but all its fcattered particles fhall be collected, and it fhall

spring

fpring forth incorruptible in immortal glory.

Chrift lives as our Redeemer, and he difcovers the glory of this his character by watching our filent remains, preferving them even in their corrupted ftate, reftoring them to their union with the foul, and raifing them fuperior to death and hell. Agreeable hereto is the infpired affertion, Hofea xiii. 14. *I will ranfom them from the power of the grave; I will redeem them from death. O death! I will be thy plague. O grave! I will be thy deftruction.*

3dly. Chrift is a victorious Redeemer. *He fhall ftand at the latter day upon the earth.* This expreffion may refer both to Chrift's incarnation, and alfo to his fecond coming without fin unto falvation.

The Old Teftament faints lived in the full expectation of the firft, and we wait for the glorious appearance of the laft. The former has fully anfwered their believing views, and we doubt not the latter will exceed all our hopes. Confidering

ing the words then as referring to the final advent of our victorious king they exprefs that glorious manifeftation which the laft great day will make, when the Lord Jefus fhall be revealed from heaven with an attending throng of mighty angels.

At prefent this character of a Redeemer is but little underftood. The glories of his redemption are degraded, his enemies feem to triumph, while by the influence of fin they endeavour to prevent the advancement of his intereft, and eclipfe the excellency of his perfon and glory; but then every ftain will be wiped off his character, and all his glories as our Redeemer will be fully difplayed, and, having vanquifhed all his enemies, and accomplifhed the purpofes of his grace, he will ftand like a conqueror upon the field of battle, furrounded with the trophies of his victory, the acclamations of his people, and the honours of an eternal triumph.

Upon the whole then we may obferve that our Redeemer's living, and ftanding

the

the latter day upon the earth affords a clear difplay of the compleatnefs of his Redemption.

Chrift would never have taken a place in heaven as the Redeemer of his people, if he had not been qualified for the work ; he never would have afcended there to make interceffion for them, if he had not perfectly accomplifhed it ; and he never would appear the fecond time, unlefs the happinefs of his people was infallibly fe-cured, for when he cometh a fecond time it is without fin unto *falvation*. His future coming therefore fuppofes the perfect accomplifhment of the redemption of his church by his firft appearance. An af-furance of the latter implies in it a cer-tainty of faith with refpect to the former, and therefore when *Job* fays he fhall ftand the latter day upon the earth he inti-mates the fatisfaction of his mind refpec-ting the perfect performance of that fal-vation, to which the character of a Re-deemer refers.

Such was the foundation upon which my dear departed friend built all his hopes,

and

and by which he was fupported with comfort in the views of eternity. Accordingly the reafon why he fixed upon this as his funeral text he has thus expreffed by writing in the paper in which it was found, " For my Funeral Text,"

" *Job*, chapter xix. verfes 25, 26, 27. " I know that my Redeemer liveth, and " that he fhall ftand at the latter day upon " the earth. And though after my fkin " worms deftroy this body, yet in my flefh " fhall I fee God. Whom I fhall fee for " myfelf, and mine eyes fhall behold, and " not another, though my reins be con- " fumed within me. It is this thought " which animates me above the fear of " dying. That Jefus died, and now he " lives, that before he expired upon the " accurfed tree he could fay, It is finifhed."

Such was the folid bafis upon which our deceafed brother refted all his expectations for an eternal world. I fhall fpend a few thoughts upon the nature of thefe expectations by proceeding to the next general propofition, which is

III. A

III. A declaration by *Job* of his hope. *Yet in my flesh shall I see God, whom I shall see for myself, and mine eyes shall behold, and not another.*

Nothing can more plainly discover the importance of the doctrines of grace than that blessed hope, which in their own nature they are calculated to inspire. Nor is there any thing can more strongly manifest the necessity of faith in this salvation than the delightful influence of its expectations upon the minds of the believer. We have an instance of this in the case of *Job.* Though one heavy affliction after another, like clouds involved in clouds, surrounded and darkened the whole sphere in which he acted, though the beating tempest poured down a flood of sorrow upon him, yet he possest his soul in patience, and uttered the language of a triumphant pleasure. Ghastly death had thinned his family. Meagre poverty had stripped him of his possessions. Dire disease had emaciated his body, and pale famine had visited his habitation, but yet, though having nothing, he seemed to possess all things.

things. Faith in a living Chrift forbids his fears, and therefore, with the gloomy horrors of the grave in profpect, he appears unfpeakably happy. What made him fo is evidently the affurance which is here expreffed. " That becaufe the " Redeemer liveth he fhould in his flefh " fee God, whom he fhould fee for him- " felf, and his eyes fhould behold, and " not another." There are two things implied in the words as conftituting the object of the hope of *Job*.

1. The refurrection of the body. *In my flefh I fhall fee God, and thefe eyes fhall behold him.* This is the antidote againft thofe painful fenfations fo naturally occafioned by the profpect of our diffolution.

" Corruption, earth, and worms,
" Shall but refine this flefh."

The believers body is only debafed, that it may be exalted. Faith in Chrift looks forward to the delightful period, when it fhall rife from the ruins of the grave, and be fafhioned like unto Chrift's glorious body.

The

The expreffion before us intimates the famenefs of that body which the refurrection fhall produce. Agreeable hereto is the infpired affertion, 1 Cor. xv. 38. " And " to every feed his own body." " My flefh, " (fays *Job*) the very fame which is now " fo emaciated, and appears fo loathfome." Though to my familiar friends it is an object of deteftation, yet it is that which God delighteth to honour. " My eyes " fhall behold him." Thefe very eyes which look upon the prefent world as a wildernefs of fin and forrow will foon be bleft with the appearance of a victorious Redeemer, and the glories of a covenant-God.

II. *Seeing God* may imply his beatific vifion. As God is the only fource of perfect happinefs to his creatures, fo the fight of him is the mean by which this blefsednefs is communicated to the mind. *The angels always behold the face of their Father which is in heaven.* * It is this which makes them happy. And the clearer the view which

D   faints

* Mat, xviii. 10.

faints upon earth obtain of the face of
God the greater is their felicity. By the
fight of God with our bodily eyes which
is here fpoken of is intimated the perfection of heavenly blifs, as infinitely fuperior
to the enjoyment of a life of faith. The
only way in which we behold God here is
by faith. Now this implies a diftance
from the great object of our pleafure, *Job*
therefore rejoices in the thought that
there fhould be no more diftance between
God and man, but that he fhould fee him
face to face. In the prefent world, while
we live by faith, we know nothing but by
report · faith gives no more than a diftant
profpect, but that in heaven will be an
immediate one. The views of faith are
often obfcured, but when in our flefh we
fhall fee God, there will be nothing to interpofe, not the leaft interruption of our
intimacy, *for we fhall know even as we are
known*.†

The language of *Job* intimates the glorified ftate of the new raifed body, *Thefe
eyes fhall behold him*. At prefent they are

unable

† 1 Cor. xiii. 12.

unable to view the illuftrious object. Its glories are fo ineffably great that were they fully manifefted, fuch is the weaknefs of our frame it would fink into ruin under the oppreffive over-whelming difplay. *No man* (fays God) *can fee me and live.* ‡ Accordingly, when *Mofes* came down from the mount he was obliged to cover his face with a veil. The reflection of that fplendor which was borrowed only from the inferior glories of Deity was too dazling for the people to behold, "So that they "were afraid to come nigh unto him ;§" but at the refurrection the cafe will be altered. *This corruptible fhall put on incorruption, and what is fown in weaknefs fhall be raifed in power.*† The body will be endowed with a divine ftrength, and fo be qualified to fuftain the weight of that glory which it fhall chearfully poffefs. Then thefe very eyes, which now cannot bear the twinkling of nature's fun, will fteadily behold the full-beaming glory of him whofe prefence irradiates heaven. *We fhall fee God.* This fight will be both

transforming

‡ Exod. xxxiii. 20. § Exod. xxxiv. 30. † 1 Cor. xv 43, 53.

transforming and tranfporting. It will transform us into his perfect image. "*We* "*fhall be like unto him, for we fhall fee as he* "*is.*"§ We fhall then alfo be freed from all that imperfection, releafed from that dulnefs and carnality, delivered from that blindnefs and corruption which now conftrain us to groan earneftly being burthened. Thus every caufe of our complaint will be removed, and we fhall be tranfported with the vifion and enjoyment of God, *whom we fhall fee for ourfelves and not another. See for ourfelves,* that is behold our intereft in him; fee him that we may enjoy him. The Lord is our portion, and this portion we fhall then fully poffefs. The faint will claim a fhare in all the glories of the divine nature. Delightful thought! while in intimate communion he fees all things in God he fhall enjoy the vaft inheritance, and with tranfporting pleafure fay, " All this is mine for " ever."

The manner in which this fight is obtained you will obferve is through the

perfon

---

§ 1 John, iii. 2

perfon of Chrift. This is intimated by the expreffion, *in my flefh,* that is, with my bodily eyes, *I fhall fee God:* now a fpiritual being is not a fuitable object for corporeal fight, and therefore the fentiment of the great Dr. *Owen* upon this fubject feems both rational and fcriptural, namely, that " A view of the glory of Chrift is " fubordinate unto the ultimate vifion of " the effence of God." The Redeemer therefore in his complex perfon will be to eternity the only mean of communication between God and the church. It is this object, the glorified body of Chrift, as fubfifting in the Godhead, which will be the medium of their knowledge, while it feafts the eyes of the countlefs multitude who furround the throne of God and the Lamb.

Application.

Hence obferve,

I. The deity of Chrift.

Seeing the Redeemer is feeing God, becaufe in him all the riches of infinite perfection are treafured up to be communicat-

ed

ed to the church. A treafure which no finite mind could poffibly contain. The capacity of the moft exalted Archangel in heaven is too limited to contain the glories of that perfection which is abfolutely immenfe, while thefe glories are therefore difplayed in the perfon of Chrift they prove his immenfity, and thus render his Deity indifputable.

2. Hence learn the neceffity of an intereft in Chrift. Life and immortality are brought to light by the gofpel, but there is no enjoying the former, or being happy in the latter, without an intereft in *Jefus*.

Sin having polluted our fouls has corrupted our bodies, and we are as unable to cleanfe the former from guilt, as to extract from the latter the feeds of our diffolution. The one muft certainly feel the influence of temporal death, and the other will as certainly be tormented with the agonies of eternal death, if Chrift is neglected and his righteoufnefs refufed.

Job had nothing to fupport him in the profpect of his diffolution but the hope

of

of feeing God, and he had nothing to fupport this hope but a knowledge of, and
dependance upon a living Redeemer.
Thus alfo it was with my dear departed
friend. He had no other expectation of
future happinefs in his dying moments,
but what arofe from the compleat redemption of the Lord Jefus Chrift. This was
revealed to him as a foundation fecure as
omnipotence could make it. It boie up
his fpirits when death entered his cham-
ber, and the grave feemed open to receive
him.

Helping to undrefs him laft Lord's-
day evening, I afked him whether he ex-
pected the reftoration of his health, or
was apprehenfive that the prefent diforder
would end in his diffolution? he anfwered, he was certain of the latter; I replied,
under the influence of this thought, that
you fhall furely die, are you happy in your
mind?—Yes, faid he, perfectly happy—
When I returned, whence does your happinefs arife? his ftrength was fo exhauft-
ed with getting into bed, that he could
only defire me to ftay for a reply, while

he

he paufed for want of breath. I waited
for a time in filent expectation; when he
began as near as I can recollect, in the following words.

"I am fenfible that I have nothing in
"myfelf to excite the divine favour, or
"merit the compaffion of God.—Was he
"this moment to fend me to the hotteft
"hell, and punifh me with eternal tor-
"ment the punifhment would not be
"too fevere: I am fully convinced it
"would be equitable. I am fenfible the
"righteoufnefs of Chrift is fufficient to
"cover all my guilt, and that on his ac-
"count God can be juft while he faves
"me. This is all my plea. From this
"arifes all my hope. I lie at the foot of
"the crofs. I know God can fave me;
"I believe he will."

Thus was he favoured in his departing
moments with the manifeftation of heavenly friendfhip, and rendered happy by
the difcoveries of redeeming love. I
mention not this circumftance to raife his
character, or to increafe that univerfal
efteem which when living he poffeft, I
only

only mention it to exalt the riches of that grace, by which he was delivered from the fears of death, and to which he afcribed all the honours of his *falvation*.

Accordingly, fpeaking of the doctrine of election the *Monday* preceding his death, he faid to a friend who vifited him, " What fhould I now do if this doctrine " was not true? The apprehenfion would " render me compleatly miferable. O how " painful my fituation now, if it was not " a certain affair, but depended upon any " thing to be done by me!—But, 'tis this " thought which fatisfies my mind in the " views of death; my falvation was be- " gun without my knowledge, and con- " trary to my inclination; it was carried " on without my aid, and perfectly finifh- " ed without my affiftance."

Upon this redemption he boldly ven- tured his foul for eternity, while he ac- knowledged it all of grace.

3. Hence learn, that the only way to obtain the fame favour is by faith in the fame Redeemer. It is not fufficient that the Son of God fuftains this character, un-

E   lef.

less we are the objects of his redeeming *love.*

Now if the word of this redemption does *not profit them that hear it,* the Apostle affirms it is *because it is not mixed with faith.*† *If we receive forgiveness of sins, and an inheritance among those that are sanctified, it is by faith in Christ,* as our Lord himself assures us.‡ While therefore we deny the efficacy of his righteousness, by depending on our own performance and seeking justification by the works of the law, we are rejecting him as a redeemer. And say, poor unbelieving sinners, what can you do without him? As a dying man I would beseech such to be reconciled to God. You believe that soon you must go the way of all flesh, do then for a few moments realize the thought of your dissolution. Your bodies are crumbled to atoms, and eaten by worms, but their scattered particles will certainly be preserved, and at the last great day collected together, but if Christ is not your redeemer, who is to raise them glorious bodies? If while living you have never given yourself up to him, when dead you

will

† Heb iv. 2. ‡ Acts xxvi. 18.

will be confidered as none of his, and at
the refurrection he will difown you, and
make this awful declaration to you,
*I know you not, depart from me all ye
workers of iniquity.** Suppofe the dying
moment arrived, and your immortal foul
taking its flight into eternity. You muft
now appear before the judgment feat of
Chrift, but how will you look him in the
face, when your own righteoufnefs has
been preferred and his neglected? How
gloomy will be your profpect in fuch a
fituation? May the Lord the fpirit affect
you with it now in fuch a manner, as fhall
conftrain you by faith *to fly to Jefus for
refuge!*

Death's terror is the mountain *faith* removes.
'Tis faith difarms deftruction, and abfolves
From ev'ry clamorous charge the guiltlefs tomb.
Believe, and fhow the reafon of a man.
Believe, and tafte the pleafures of a God;
Believe, and look with triumph on the tomb.

YOUNG.

4thly. We may hence learn the excellency of an affurance that we are interefted in Chrift. While mankind would not
venture half their worldly fubftance in any
fcheme

scheme which they had not good evidence
would succeed, they willingly venture their
immortal souls, their eternal happiness
with dark uncertainty, destitute of the
least evidence of their safety. With how
many is this the melancholy case? Or
how many are there who foolishly raise
their hopes without any foundation, and
indulge a blind expectation which is void
of all support? What confusion will fill
the minds of such, when their eyes are
open by death, and they see themselves
exposed to the wrath of an eternal God,
destitute of any shelter, any hope? Hence
my dear friends, learn the necessity of a
continual inquiry what is your state towards God. Swift as a post you are daily
hastening to an eternal world. Let con-
science hourly put the question, " Am I
" travelling to the dark regions of end-
" less torment? or am I daily approach-
" ing the gates of immortal light and
" blessedness?" The importance of such
an inquiry appears from the realizing
views of a dying moment. 'Tis then we
shall feel the necessity of having made *our
calling and election sure.** Supposing we

really

* 1 Pet. i. 1:.

really are fafe, yet to be in the dark in that moment is to fuffer awhile the torments of the damned.

Ye drowfy profeffors! the death-bed of my dear friend calls loudly upon you, and in awful language reads the moft important lecture. It tells you eternity is upon the wing, and calls your attention to an endlefs duration. *The day is far fpent, the night is at hand, let us put off the works of darknefs, and put on the whole armour of light.*†

The dear deceafed knew the importance of this affurance to which I am now preffing you. In his dying moments he appeared a lively inftance of the poffibility of attaining it, for then he enjoyed that folid comfort which it affords, while he could fay with *Job, I know that my Redeemer liveth.* It was this which compofed his mind, and infpired his heart with joy. Nor was his joy the effect of agitated fpirits or fluctuating paffions, but the refult of a calm reflection upon his ftate towards God, *as not having on his own righteoufnefs which is of the law, but clothed with the righteoufnefs of Chrift which is by faith.*§

† Rom. xiii. 12. § Phil. ii. 9.

The frame of his mind is beft defcribed by himfelf in a paper found in his pocket the night preceding his death, of which the following is an exact copy. —" The " following thoughts occurred to me, " when death appeared in profpect. They " contain my hopes and my fears at a " time I had not the leaft expectation of " life. In fhort I found fuch reflections " of infinite fervice. My mind became " more unbent from terreftrial things. " The world vanifhed, and my happinefs " was derived from objects unfeen and " eternal. I could converfe familiarly with " death and eternity. I could ftrictly " examine the dark dungeon of my own " heart. I could read my Bible with " more earneftnefs and pleafure, as I con- " fidered myfelf interefted in every fen- " tence; and, when faith was in exercife, " I could fay, *my beloved is mine, and I* " *am his.* I was happy in myfelf, and " happy in the thoughts of my approach- " ing diffolution."

Thoughts on DEATH and ETERNITY.

" I fee the hour approach, th' important hour,
" And death commiffion'd, ready to devour,

" Now

" Now med'cine fails, and phyfic cannot fave
" From death's black horrors, and the rav'nous
    grave.

" Reflect, my foul, and think what 'tis to die :
" One fatal ftroke diffolves the tender tye :
" Tir'd with it's prifon, cumber'd with it's clay,
" The long-imprifon'd fpirit foars away.

" Now fkulls and coffins open to my view,
" The yawning grave clofe by the baleful yew,
" Confin'd to dwell within the hollow ground,
" While worms, and bones, and fpectres me fur-
    round.

" And can we view thy trophies, death, nor fear ?
" Feel life decay, nor drop a filent tear ?
" Methinks a few more days will end the ftrife ·
" Death hovers near to fnap the thread of life.

" But rife, my foul, and all the world refign,
" *Jefus* appears with marks of blood divine :
" I plead that blood, my prophet, prieft and king,
" The grave lies conquer'd, death has loft its
    fting.

" Then earth farewell, thou flattering world adieu:
" Sublimer pleafures open to my view :
" Of

" Of joys fubftantial is my foul poffeft,
" And fongs of angels fire my raptur'd breaft."

The whole ftrain of his difcourfe with
me was exactly coincident with the fen-
timents here expreffed. Throughout his
illnefs the adverfary of fouls was kept
at a diftance from him; or if in any inftance his approach was permitted, it
was not to attack the foundation of his
hope, but only to diftrefs him with the
fear that it was poffible, notwithftanding
his affurance, he had never built upon it.
A fear this which the hypocrite is fel-
dom troubled with, for he is too much in
love with his delufion.

Converfing with me about the trying
moment, I repeated to him thofe en-
couraging promifes, Deut. xxxiii. 5. *As
thy day is, fo fhall thy ftrength be.* Heb.
xiii. 5. *I will never leave thee, I will never
forfake thee.* I obferved from them that
God beftows the favours of his love but
when the circumftances of his people
renders them abfolutely neceffary, and only gives them ftrength anfwerable to their
prefent trial, and when death comes they
fhall find grace fufficient for the day.

With

With an expreffive chearfulnefs he
looked me in the face, and readily replied,
" I do believe it. I have thus far found
" it fo, and I have no doubt that I fhall
" ftill experience it to be the cafe."
Thus he trufted in the Lord that he
would deliver him, and his example il-
luftrated the truth of the divine promife,
I. Peter ii. 5. *He that believeth in him fhall
not be confounded.*

Accordingly within an hour of his
death with a faultering tongue he de-
fired his weeping father to go to prayer
with him. After prayer he was afked
if he remembered one of the promifes
before referred to, and what he now
thought concerning it? He replied he
did, and his thoughts were the fame now
as before. His experience thus gave teftimony to the faithfulnefs of a performing
God, and therefore with ferenity on his
countenance, and without a figh, he
clofed his eyes in death, and faw his Redeemer in glory.

Is there not reafon then to congratulate
the mourning parents and affectionate re-
latives of this bleffed faint? In that glory
doubtlefs he is. God has put a diftin-

F   guifhed

guifhed honour upon you his parents.
Under your care he was trained up for
the kingdom of glory, and now is in the
full poffeffion of its unbounded pleafures.
Indulge therefore the pleafing thought of
his prefent fituation, *and forrow not as
thofe who have no hope.* § The mortal
part of your child it is true is dead, but
your Redeemer liveth. In him is a fuffi-
ciency to make up the lofs, and he lives
to fupport you under it.

I almoft fear addreffing myfelf to the
furviving brothers and fifter of the dear
deceafed. Their tender paffions I know
are fuch that they can hardly bear it.
You have my affectionate fympathy while
I feel for myfelf, but permit me to obferve that when grief is immoderate it
is offenfive to the eyes of God, and may
provoke him to repeat the painful ftroke.
'Tis your duty therefore to endeavour
to check the gufhes of paffion, and keep
it within its due bounds. Be earneft in
your applications to a throne of grace,
and feek for relief to a covenant-God,
who has gracioufly declared for the comfort of his people *that in all their afflicti-*
ons

§ 1 Thef. iv. 14.

ons he is afflicted.† You loved your brother. Where would love wish him but in a world of ineffable blifs? Surely the confideration of his happinefs then muft afford you real pleafure! Inftead of pondering therefore upon the painful truth *that he is abfent from the body,* whenever you remember him admit the foul-reviving truth, *that he is prefent with the Lord.*‡ If his company afforded you pleafure upon earth be concerned to follow him fo far as he followed Chrift, left an eternal feparation fhould aggravate your prefent diftrefs by the defpairing reflections of eternal mifery. Nothing but an intereft in the fame Saviour who has redeemed his foul from the dreadful confequences of fin can fecure and comfort you in a dying hour.

It gives me pleafure to hope that you are convinced of this, and that the prefent affliction has increafed your defires after the one thing needful, and it is my prayer fuch defires may never be extinguifhed. *There is a friend remaineth that fticketh clofer than a brother,* § who is both able and willing to fatisfy them.

If

† Ifaiah liii. 9   ‡ 2 Cor. v. 8   § Prov. xviii. 24.

If the prefent afflictive ftroke is a mean of increafing your intimacy with him you will have reafon to fay, " It was " good for us that we were afflicted." ||

I cannot pafs unnoticed the affectionate relative, whofe vifit has been attended with fuch contrary fcenes You came here in full expectation of pleafure, but the moft diftreffing pains have difappointed your hope, and caft a tremendous gloom upon the enjoyments of friendfhip. This, my dear friend, is only a fpecimen of what you are continually to meet with while paffing through life, and while the prefent providence teaches the vanity of all earthly pleafure it loudly calls upon you to feek thofe things which are above. Nothing but the delights of the heavenly world can afford you folid hap-pinefs; and nothing but the well-ground-ed hopes of them can fupport you under the diftreffes of the prefent life. You are taught by the death of your friend that the only way to obtain this felicity is by faith in a living Redeemer. 'Tis my fer-vent prayer that the inftruction may not be in vain.

But

|| Pfalm cxix. 71.

But the providence which occasions
the solemnities of this day is also affecti-
onately felt and sincerely mourned by
the family present who stand in a nearer
relation to the deceased. It is to you my
friends like the knife of a surgeon laying
open an old wound. It revives the remem-
brance of former sorrows, while every
circumstance attending the preceding
breach in your family is mustered up

 By busy meddling memory
 In barbarous succession.

I sincerely feel for you under the painful trials, but God is still the same, and
the affection of a Redeemer is able to
relieve you. 'Tis my hope and prayer
that, while your afflictions are repeated,
and the clouds return after the rain, you
may fly to a covenant God for refuge,
obtain the possession of spiritual consolation, converse with heavenly realities,
experience the anticipations of future
glory, and an increasing preparation for
the inheritance of the saints in light.

But is not the death of our friend,
which is so universally lamented a common

mon lofs, by which we are each one of us addreffed with the folemn advice. " *Prepare to meet thy God.*" ‡ In a particular manner it conveys a moft ftriking lecture to the younger part of this congregation. It teaches the uncertainty of life, it fhews what Chriftianity can do, and urges an immediate application to the Lord Jefus Chrift. If youth, good natural abilities, a friendly difpofition, and a temper univerfally amiable could fecure from the ftroke of death our deceafed brother had been now alive.

If natural qualifications and moral performances could of themfelves intitle to the divine favour, you will all of you acknowledge there would have been no neceffity for him to have renounced himfelf, and made the righteoufnefs of Chrift his only plea.

Hence then you may learn the uncertainty of creature-enjoyments, and the abfolute neceffity of an appropriating faith in a living Redeemer. 'Tis this alone which can render us comfortable while furrounded with the numerous ills which flefh is heir to. 'Tis this alone can compofe the fpirits in a dying moment,

‡ Amos iv. 12.

ment, and caufe us to triumph over the grave.

There are many of you did in reality love him. His departure has affected you with a conviction how vain are the expectations of earthly happinefs, and I hope revived in your minds a fenfe of the neceffity of an intereft in eternal felicity.

If deftitute of the influence of the fpirit fuch impreffions will be tranfitory, and when time fhall fet the providence at a diftance they will be worn away. O then pray to God that they may be effectual and lafting! It would be dreadful indeed, if after fuch a warning as this, you fhould return *as the dog to his vomit, or the fow that was wafhed to her wallowing in the mire.* *

O then be concerned to guard against fuch an iffue, and pray, I fay again, that your prefent convictions may never die away, but that you may continually feel the influence of that important advice, which this difpenfation fpeaks, and is fpoken alfo in the language of infpiration. " Gird up the loins of your minds,§ " be fober, be vigilant; for your adver-
" fory,

* 2 Pet. ii. 22. § 1 Pet 1. 13.

" fary, the devil, goeth about as a roaring
" lion, seeking whom he may devour."[†]
Upon the whole then

Our Redeemer liveth, and he shall stand
the latter day upon the earth. That day
is fast approaching. Let us anticipate its
joys while we indulge the pleasing expectation. Thus animated we shall become
superior to all the light afflictions of time.
They are but momentary compared with
future glory.

It is but a night, a dark and moonless
night which will usher in eternal day.

Delightful consideration that our redeemer lives and will soon appear, with a
glorious retinue of saints and angels ! Our
dear friend I doubt not will make one of
his train. We shall then see him not
afflicted with pale disease, nor disfigured
by emaciating sickness, but clothed with
immortal life, chearfulness in his countenance, joy inspiring his heart, and his per-
son adorned with the bright splendor of
eternal glory. Happy meeting! never
more to be separated.—*For so shall we ever
be with the Lord* [‡]

[†] 1 Pet v. 8. [‡] 1 Thef iv. 17.

F I N I S.

CPSIA information can be obtained at www.ICGtesting.com
Printed in the USA
BVOW06s1442060214

344166BV00008B/197/P

9 781170 481936